Stuntology

DISCARD

Stuntology® ©2002 by Sam Bartlett

Stuntology Press
333 South Jackson
Bloomington, IN, 47403
(812) 330-8731
sambartlett.com

Cover design by Merridee LaMantia
Cover photo by Abby Ladin

Printed in the USA

ISBN 1-885387-09-1

Copyright 2002, 2003 by Sam Bartlett

For Abby

Chaos, Pandemonium, and the Art of Flirtation:
An Introduction to *Stuntology*

You have in your hands something the likes of which you've never seen—something remarkable, unfamiliar and strange. Introductions are in order.

First, the work itself:

Extravagant Claim #1: Samuel Bartlett's *Stuntology* is the latest arrival in a grand cavalcade of American iconoclasm. Benjamin Franklin, Henry David Thoreau, e.e. cummings, Alexander Calder, The Three Stooges, Rube Goldberg and R. Crumb are its progenitors. The traditions are irreverence and boldness, a freedom to make new forms, and an uncontrollable urge to alter human behavior.

Extravagant Claim #2: Like *Poor Richard's Almanac*, *Life in The Woods*, Calder's mobiles, and the horseplay of Larry, Moe and Curly, *Stuntology* invites us to use the stuff of everyday life to transform ordinary existence into a utopia – in this case a surreal utopia of terrifying comic potential. Pieces of spaghetti, shoved inside a watermelon, become worms; a drive home with friends on a dark road, an opportunity for psychic torture; and a lovely breakfast of pancakes, an occasion for digestive chaos. Best of all *Stuntology* shows you how to do it yourself. It belongs on a shelf alongside *The Whole Earth Catalog* and *The Official Boy Scout Handbook*.

Extravagant Claim #3: *Stuntology* is more subversive — and American – than the only comparable guide to clandestine behavior, *Max and Mauritz*. In the German children's classic by Walter Busch, two wicked boys play seven instructive, illustrated tricks before they're caught and ground to flour. But Bartlett's top-hatted merry prankster always gets away with it. He's the mad uncle of your dreams. Read his adventures and neither he nor you ever grow up or get caught.

And now, to the author.

Biographical Exhibit #1: Generally regarded as a healthy young Vermonter, Samuel Bartlett collapsed one day while still in the second grade. Head against standard-issue desk. An alarming klonk.

He was sent home in agony, clutching his abdomen, barely

able to speak. His mother put him to bed. He could offer no explanation for his condition. It was: a mystery. Until Mrs. Bartlett discovered, in the wastebasket near his bedroom desk, an empty bag of prunes. Questioning revealed he had eaten the entire bag— as an experiment.

Biographical Exhibit #2: As a teenager Bartlett showed up unannounced at my house one summer's day behind the wheel of a convertible Triumph sports car, 1960's vintage. The car belonged to the boyfriend of one of his three older sisters; said boyfriend had spent months restoring it to working order before making the generous but critical mistake of loaning it to Bartlett for a drive 'round Vermont's back roads. (For those interested in the effects of birth order on the human imagination, Sam is the youngest of four siblings and the only boy.)

Immediately, we tried to think of a girl sporting enough to get in the car with us, but not so sporting she couldn't be easily terrified. We came up with three. They were all home. One by one, we collected them and tore around, spinning out at dirt road intersections, pretending to lose the steering on dangerous turns, complaining the brakes were malfunctioning as we plunged down Church Hill. Primal flirtation. The sort of flirtation boys first employ when, answering a primitive urge, they choose to punch the girl they like the most on the arm. Sam returned the Triumph at dusk. To the best of our knowledge it never ran again.

Biographical Exhibit #3: Growing up amidst the rough and tumble of rural New Englanders, Bartlett opted for the path less traveled and did not drink, smoke cigarettes or consume illegal drugs during his high school days at Champlain Valley Union in Hinesburg, Vermont. That changed on a trip to the European continent where, after graduating, he set out to encounter the great works of art and architecture. We eventually made our way to a small pension in Venice. I had to take an overnight train trip to Munich. Bartlett remained behind.

In my absence he chose to eschew St. Mark's Cathedral and the Grand Canal and decided instead to find out what all the fuss was about getting drunk. After a hearty spaghetti dinner, he purchased a bottle of inexpensive Chianti and a large rubber ball, locked the door to our room and holed up for the night. His exploration of the effects of alcohol on human loco-motor functions was methodical. He bounced the ball against the pension's wall, testing his reflexes, as he worked his way through the entire liter of cheap red wine.

The results of the experiment were spectacular, as the owner of the pension, who was most concerned about Sam's condition — and the condition of the room he had rented us — showed me when I returned the next morning. We toured the wreckage and gingerly roused Signor Bartlett, still ignorant of the beauties of Venice, but a wiser and paler young American.

*

QED, the author of *Stuntology* has long relished the following:

- a diabolic lust for experiment,
- the comedy of human suffering,
- the anarchic joy of destruction,
- and the willful pandemonium that lies in the heart of flirtation.

As to Mr. Bartlett's current whereabouts—they're difficult to ascertain. He is known to be an itinerant musician and regular traveler. But as the volume you hold demonstrates, he is at heart an inveterate trickster. In my mind he's forever out there, perhaps at some crackpot *Stuntology* test facility near Bloomington, Indiana, trying out new stunts for you and me. Wheeeeehaaaaaa!

— Theodore E. Braun III, B.A., M.F.A., D.S.
(Doctor of Stuntology)
Senior Lecturer in Screenwriting
School of Cinema-Television
University of Southern California

Acknowledgments

Very special thanks to Jim Bardwell, Dave Barry, Richmond Bartlett, Miki Bird, Ted Braun, Malcolm Dalglish, Jane Hamilton, Rob Hayes, John Herrmann, Kevin Kelly, Abby Ladin, Merridee LaMantia, Robert Meitus, Dee Mortensen, Lisa Nilsson, Danny Noveck, Rich Remsberg, Elka and Peter Schumann, Ned Shaw, Sue Sternberg, Karen Strum, and Steve Volan.

— S.B., October 2001

WATERMELON STUNT ✦

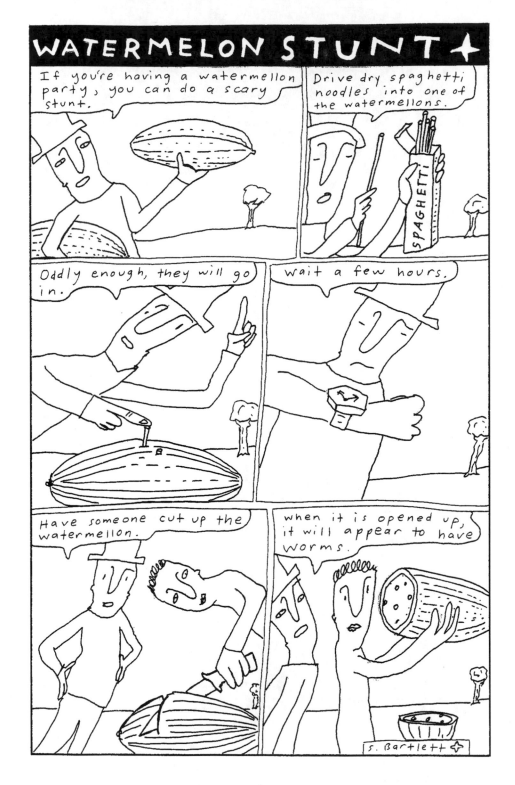

FINGER FOOD ✦

A guy came up to me in montana. He had a toothpick jabbed completely through his index finger.

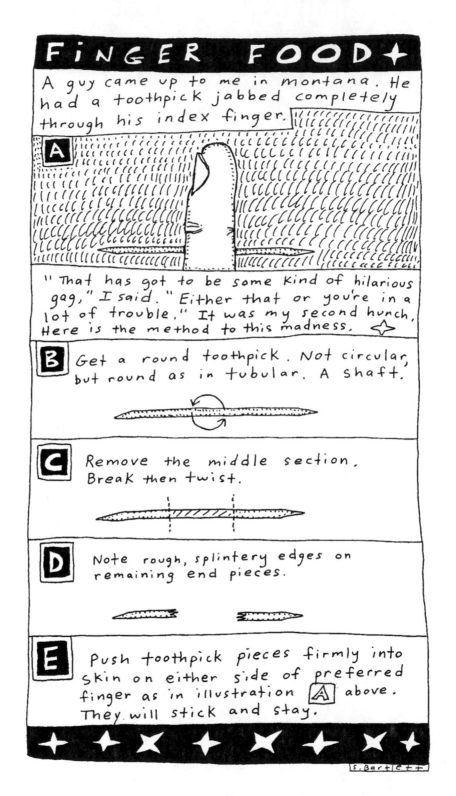

A

"That has got to be some kind of hilarious gag," I said. "Either that or you're in a lot of trouble." It was my second hunch. Here is the method to this madness. ✧

B Get a round toothpick. Not circular, but round as in tubular. A shaft.

C Remove the middle section. Break then twist.

D Note rough, splintery edges on remaining end pieces.

E Push toothpick pieces firmly into skin on either side of preferred finger as in illustration A above. They will stick and stay.

S. Bartlett

6

resurrect a chicken
To do this you will need a towel.
A man ran over a chicken with his car. The chicken was flattened, seemingly beyond repair, but then another man came up and said, "I can fix this chicken."
The man took the flattened chicken, which we will represent as a towel, and he rolled it widthwise toward the center from each end.
Then he folded it in half so the flat parts met. This made the chicken appear to have four sections.
[top view]
Next, he pulled the corner ends of the towel from the center of each of the four sections, so they protruded.
Then he pinched the opposite little tips of towel and pulled in the indicated direction, which is really the only direction the towel will go.
And voila! he had a flattened chichen puffed back to life.
S. Bartlett

18

GOODBYE ✦

teeth

I've researched a lot of variations of this trick. Here's my current favorite:

Fill your mouth with Altoid mints.

Go to a crowded thoroughfare.

Pretend to walk straight into a lamp-post. Kick the base of it so it goes, "Glinggg!"

Spit out your Altoids one by one, clutching your mouth and saying a muffled "oh my god," and "ouch."

S. Bartlett

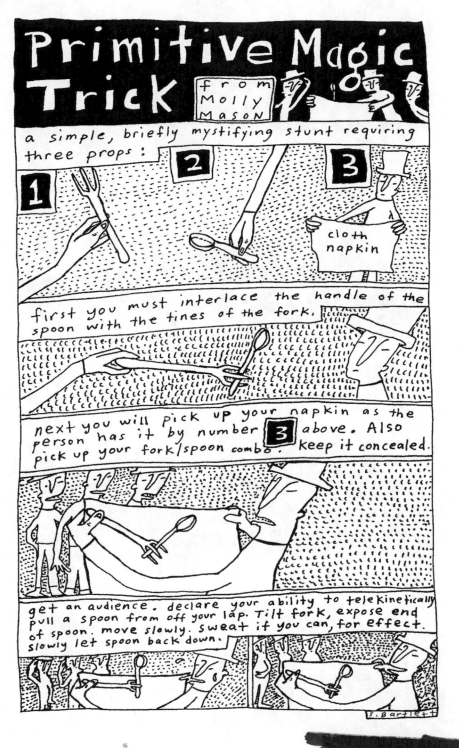

Dandelion Magnetism

"Good to play on someone with a good sense of humor or someone who already regards themself as a victim," writes sherry Frazer, who does this trick.

you need: a dandelion flower, a dandelion seed head, and a fool.

The dialogue might go something like this:

Did you know that you can hide a dandelion flower _anywhere_ on your body and the seed head can always find it?

This seems impossible to me but I'm willing to go along with it for the purposes of this cartoon.

Go ahead. Try it. I won't look. (and you don't have to)

He hides it in his shoe.

Now, with the seed head, carefully move around the surface of his body, pausing here and there. [try to avoid any place the flower might actually be] vibrate the seed head a little from time to time. Finally you come to the mouth...

It's not in your mouth is it?

They open their mouth wide to show how empty it is, and then in goes the seed head, wiggle-wiggle: dandelion fluff all over their bicuspids and uvula. Ha ha ha.

S. Bartlett

Have you felt my wart?

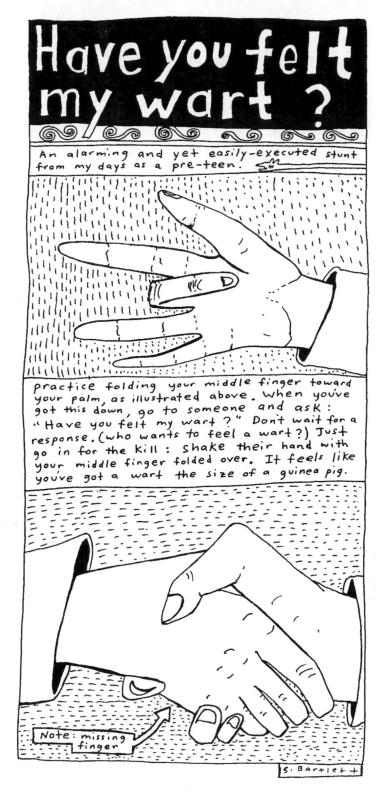

An alarming and yet easily-executed stunt from my days as a pre-teen.

practice folding your middle finger toward your palm, as illustrated above. When you've got this down, go to someone and ask: "Have you felt my wart?" Don't wait for a response. (who wants to feel a wart?) Just go in for the kill: shake their hand with your middle finger folded over. It feels like you've got a wart the size of a guinea pig.

Note: missing finger

S. Bartlett

Siamese Belts

You can join belts with someone for fun and injury.

First of all, how much do you value your belt-loops? Do you know how to sew?

Ok, stand front-to-front with your future siamese belts partner

Unhook your belts then hook them with your partner. Your buckle will go with their belt-end. Their buckle will go with your belt-end.

Top view

The final step is to begin sprinting and spinning and leaping together as one lunatic creature.

You might want to get your belt out from under these loops in front.
It will be a little more comfortable when you begin gyrating

S. Bartlett

SHRILL STRAW

First, let me apply fair warning: I've gotten myself in trouble with this trick. The chances are you will too. O.K., go ahead.

Get yourself a glass of water and a straw. That's all you'll need.

Do I need to state the obvious? This is a restaurant stunt, good in all restaurants in the lower 48.

allright, so what you do next is suck some water into the straw and then pinch the end so the water can't escape.

Suck   **Pinch**

Now pucker up your embouchere and blow across the end of the straw while simultaneously letting the water out of the straw with your pinch hand. Let the water out slowly for best results. It should sound like a very shrill slide whistle, only louder. With the right straw you can get a sound so piercing and screachy that people will get angry at you, especially after the 69th repetition.

1. suck 2. pinch 3. blow

thankyou Susan Murphy

S. Bartlett

26

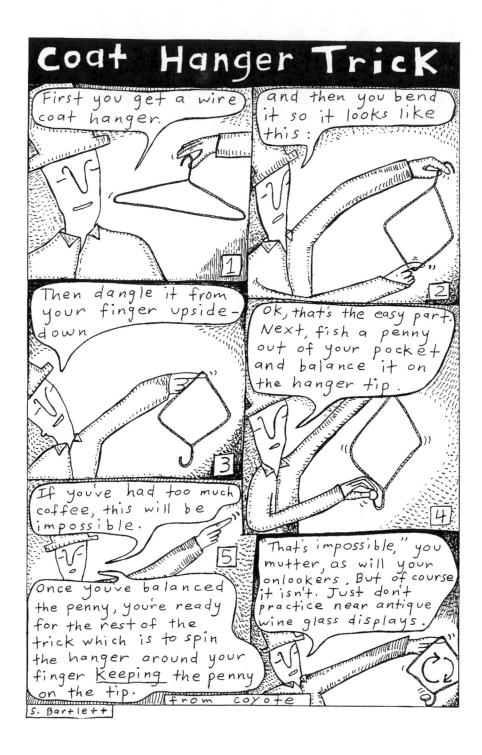

Coat Hanger Trick

1. First you get a wire coat hanger.

2. and then you bend it so it looks like this:

3. Then dangle it from your finger upside-down

4. Ok, that's the easy part. Next, fish a penny out of your pocket and balance it on the hanger tip.

5. If you've had too much coffee, this will be impossible.

Once you've balanced the penny, you're ready for the rest of the trick which is to spin the hanger around your finger <u>keeping</u> the penny on the tip.

"That's impossible," you mutter, as will your onlookers. But of course it isn't. Just don't practice near antique wine glass displays.

S. Bartlett

from coyote

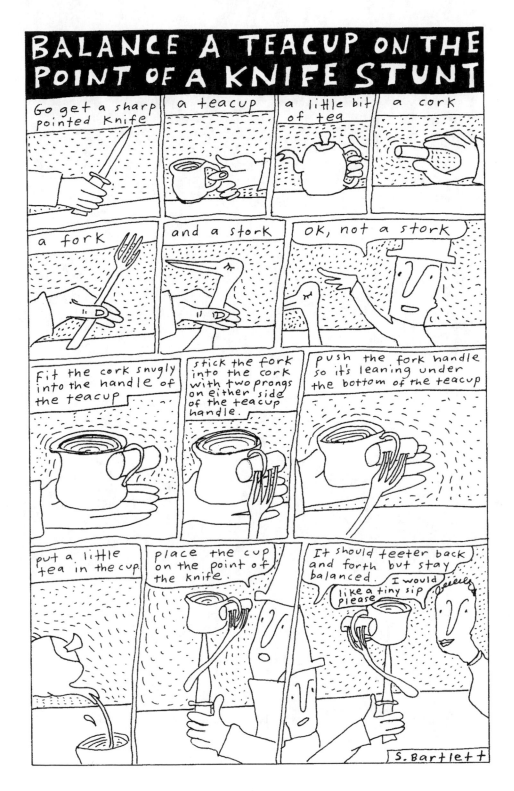

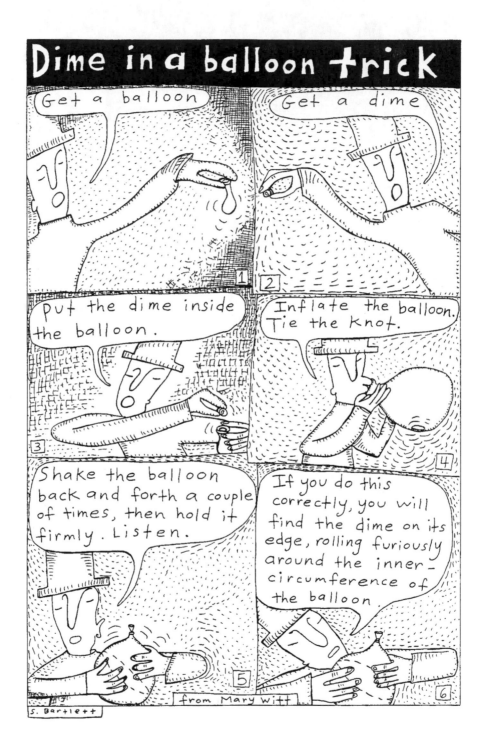

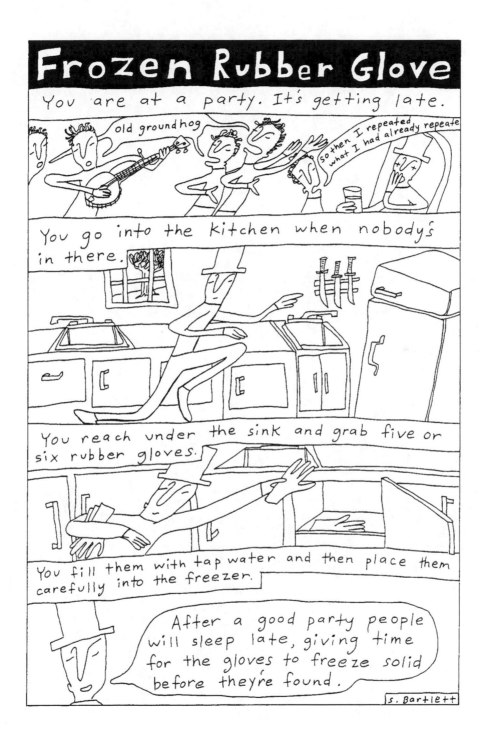

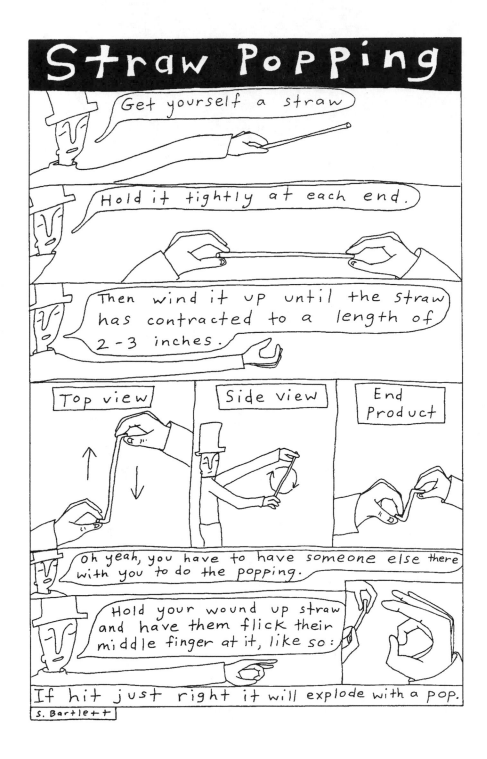

39

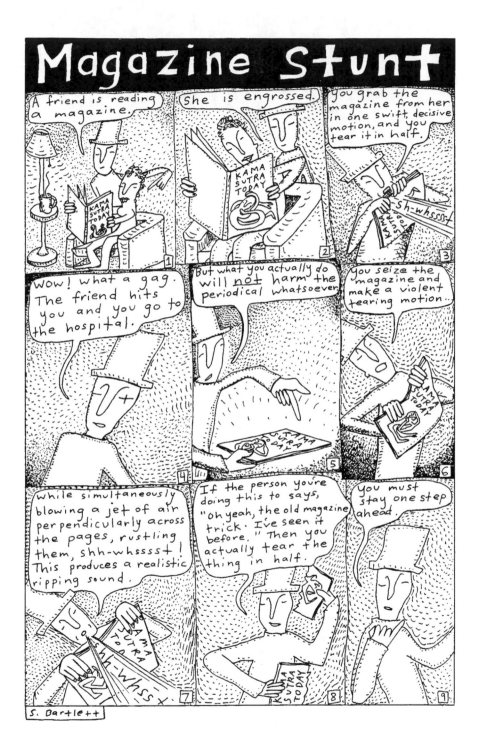

BATHROOM STUNT

Over a course of several weeks or months enter the bathroom while your sibling is in the shower.

Develop a pattern of your normal presence in the bathroom while this person showers, so you being there is not a cause for suspicion.

Then one day fill a big cup with ice-cold water while said sibling is showering,

and nonchalantly pour the cup of cold water over the curtain and onto your unfortunate victim's hind and front quarters.

Aiiiiiiiiiiii!!

from Eve Podet   S. Bartlett

Roller Shade Sabotage

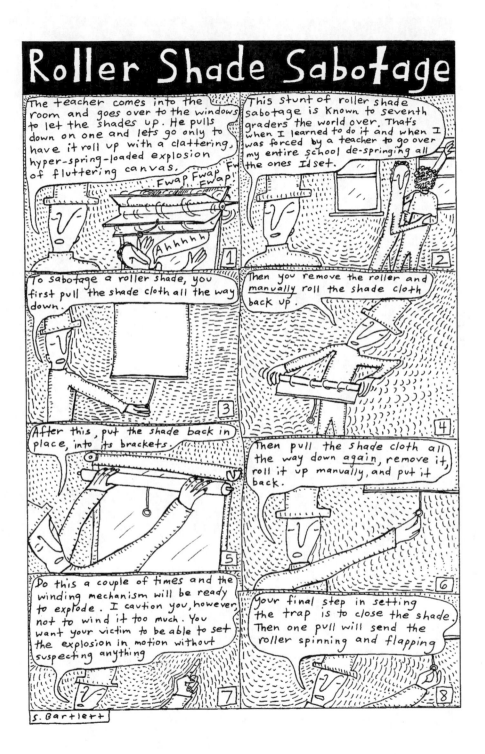

The teacher comes into the room and goes over to the windows to let the shades up. He pulls down on one and lets go only to have it roll up with a clattering, hyper-spring-loaded explosion of fluttering canvas.

Fwap Fwap Fw

Ahhhhh

1

This stunt of roller shade sabotage is known to seventh graders the world over. That's when I learned to do it and when I was forced by a teacher to go over my entire school de-springing all the ones I set.

2

To sabotage a roller shade, you first pull the shade cloth all the way down.

3

Then you remove the roller and *manually* roll the shade cloth back up.

4

After this, put the shade back in place, into its brackets.

5

Then pull the shade cloth all the way down *again*, remove it, roll it up manually, and put it back.

6

Do this a couple of times and the winding mechanism will be ready to explode. I caution you, however, not to wind it too much. You want your victim to be able to set the explosion in motion without suspecting anything

7

Your final step in setting the trap is to close the shade. Then one pull will send the roller spinning and flapping

8

S. Bartlett

FOOD·CONCEALING STUNT

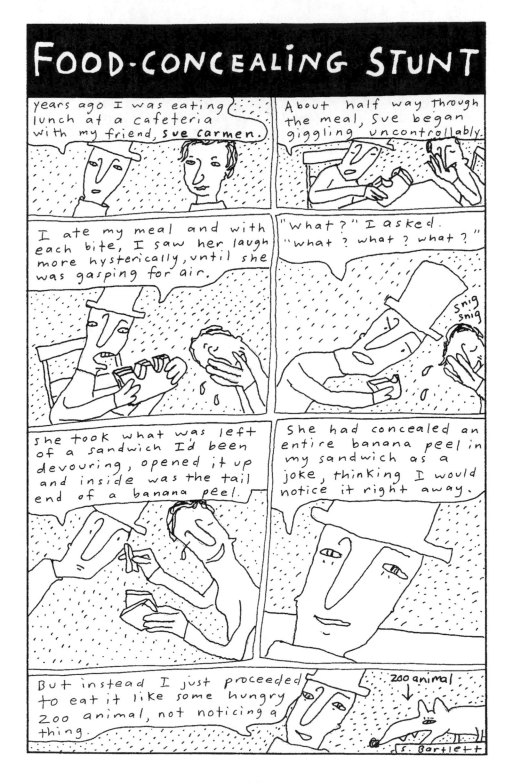

years ago I was eating lunch at a cafeteria with my friend, **sue carmen**.

About half way through the meal, sue began giggling uncontrollably.

I ate my meal and with each bite, I saw her laugh more hysterically, until she was gasping for air.

"what?" I asked. "what? what? what?"

snig snig

she took what was left of a sandwich I'd been devouring, opened it up and inside was the tail end of a banana peel.

She had concealed an entire banana peel in my sandwich as a joke, thinking I would notice it right away.

But instead I just proceeded to eat it like some hungry zoo animal, not noticing a thing.

zoo animal →

S. Bartlett

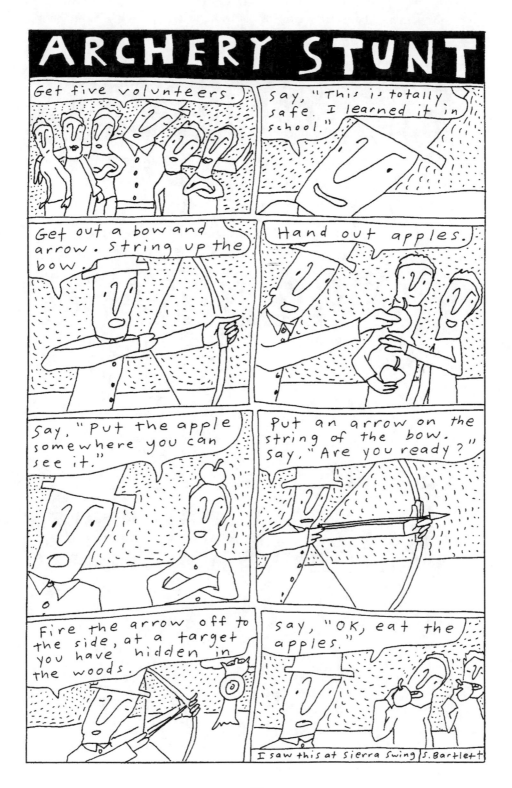

ventriloquism at tollbooths

Requires: one person hidden behind the driver's seat and another person (the driver) who will mouth the words.

Also: you'll need an audience in the rest of the vehicle to watch the performance.

So, you've pulled up to the tollbooth and the tollbooth operator says:

That'll be a dollar fifty ma'am.

and you the driver begin moving your lips while the hidden "ventriloquist" says:

How do I get to the nearest diner? Thankyou for your help. Have a good day.

S. Bartlett

52

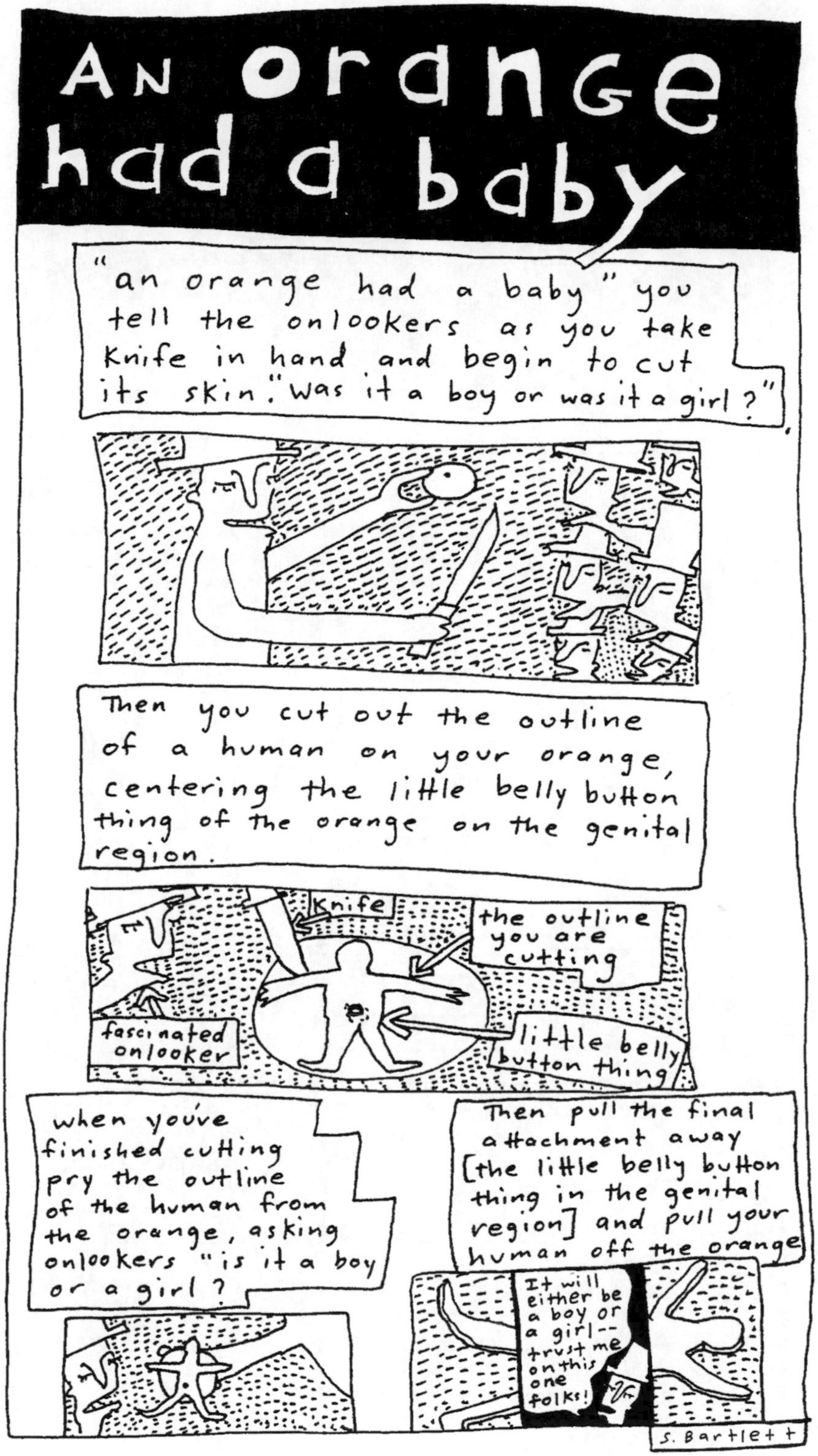

An orange had a baby

"an orange had a baby" you tell the onlookers as you take knife in hand and begin to cut its skin. "Was it a boy or was it a girl?"

Then you cut out the outline of a human on your orange, centering the little belly button thing of the orange on the genital region.

knife

the outline you are cutting

fascinated onlooker

little belly button thing

when you've finished cutting pry the outline of the human from the orange, asking onlookers "is it a boy or a girl?

Then pull the final attachment away [the little belly button thing in the genital region] and pull your human off the orange

It will either be a boy or a girl— trust me on this one folks!

S. Bartlett

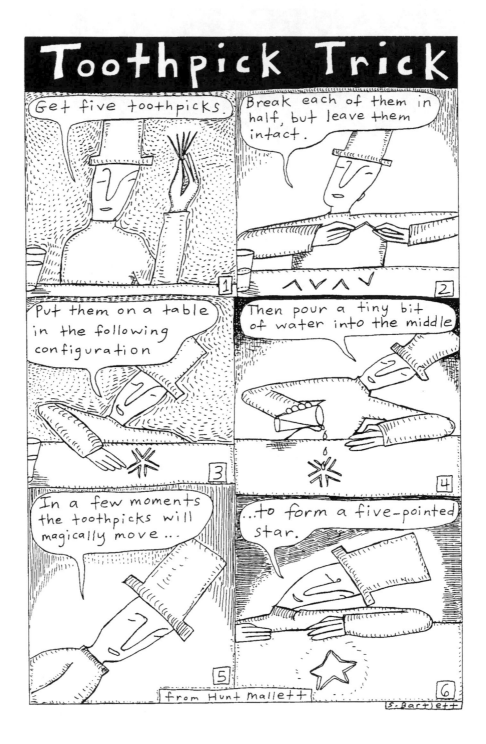

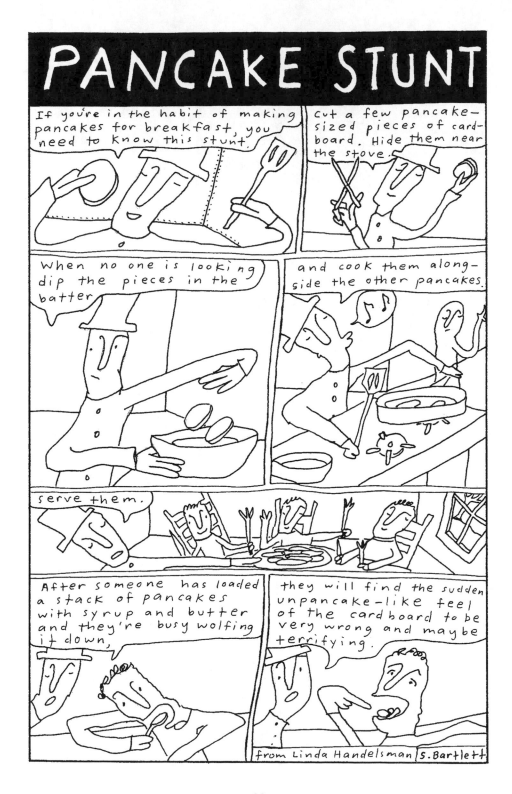

STUNT
face-slapping

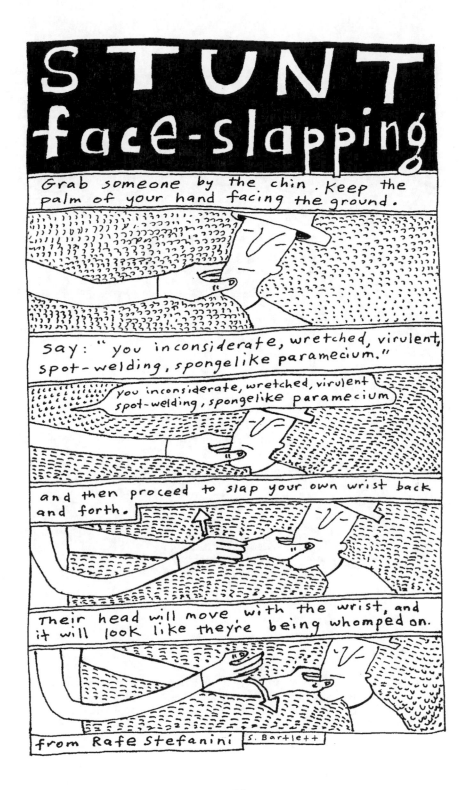

Grab someone by the chin. Keep the palm of your hand facing the ground.

Say: "you inconsiderate, wretched, virulent, spot-welding, spongelike paramecium."

you inconsiderate, wretched, virulent spot-welding, spongelike paramecium

and then proceed to slap your own wrist back and forth.

Their head will move with the wrist, and it will look like they're being whomped on.

from Rafe Stefanini   S. Bartlett

styrofoam cup + mouth-enhancer

1 Get a styrofoam cup.

2 Poke out the bottom.

3 Stick the large end into your mouth so the rim of the cup is between your lips and your gums. This is a little tricky at first.

4 The inner parts of your mouth will be put on display. They will look slightly larger and slightly scarier than they actually are.

5 Put on some sort of mouth show for someone.

S. Bartlett

Pre-Sliced Banana

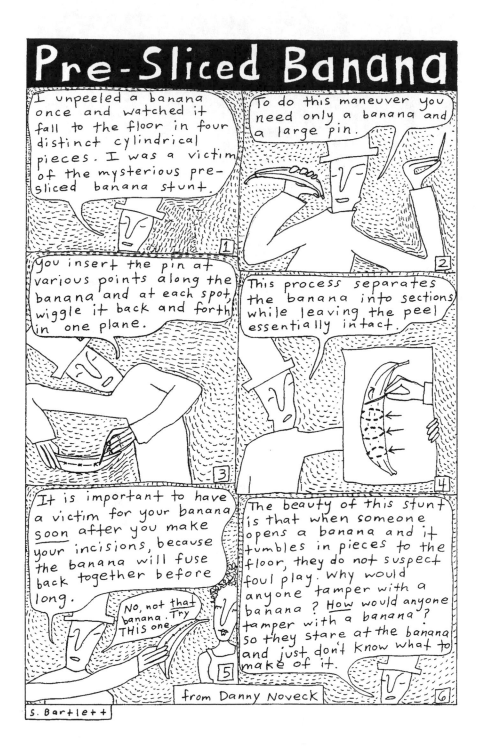

1. I unpeeled a banana once and watched it fall to the floor in four distinct cylindrical pieces. I was a victim of the mysterious pre-sliced banana stunt.

2. To do this maneuver you need only a banana and a large pin.

3. You insert the pin at various points along the banana and at each spot, wiggle it back and forth in one plane.

4. This process separates the banana into sections while leaving the peel essentially intact.

5. It is important to have a victim for your banana soon after you make your incisions, because the banana will fuse back together before long.

No, not that banana. Try THIS one.

6. The beauty of this stunt is that when someone opens a banana and it tumbles in pieces to the floor, they do not suspect foul play. Why would anyone tamper with a banana? How would anyone tamper with a banana? So they stare at the banana and just don't know what to make of it.

from Danny Noveck

S. Bartlett

72

Pistachio Trick

The pistachio is a tree-bearing, iron-shelled, edible nut with a green interior.

In every bag of pistachios there are about 28 that haven't cracked open in the roasting process.

28

one pistachio bag →

Well, you have two options.

You can crack them open with your teeth and in the process, inadvertently moosh together the shards of shell and the kernel, and then try to separate them with your tongue, and then swallow the mess, causing great damage to your intestines.

Or you can save these closed pistachios for about a year, and then serve them in a bowl at a party.

Then watch people, starved for pistachios, rifling through the bowl for a single edible pistachio. It will be like a bad dream, effective against both the rubber glove guy and the label remover

S. Bartlett

Impossible Cork Stunt

This is a party trick. You'll need an empty bottle of wine and its cork.

challenge someone to shove the cork back into the bottle. All the way in. They might think this is the stunt.

After they've done it, you tell them, "I can remove the cork using only this cloth napkin." (hopefully it's a nice party and there are cloth napkins all over the place.)

You prepare the napkin by folding two of the ends towards the middle.

Le voila!

Put one tip of the folded napkin into the wine bottle. Get the cork to rest in the middle of the cloth, a few inches from the end.

When the cork is positioned pull slowly and firmly. The cork will come out with the napkin.

from Barbara Lubell

J. Bartlett

84

Straw Zurna

from chuck Corman and Becky Ashenden

You will need a plastic straw and a swiss Army knife with scissors.

information corner ◇◇◇◇
A zurna? It's a very loud traditional wind instrument.

First you will flatten one end of the straw.

Before

After

Next you will cut two pieces from the flattened end of the straw.

Before

After

Now put the pointy end into your mouth about an inch, so it can freely vibrate.

Before

After

press down on the straw with your lips. Be firm, but don't flatten the straw completely.

As you blow, you'll feel the tip vibrate in your mouth.

Cut finger holes. (not too close to the mouth-piece) Experiment with different straw lengths.

Remember: two zurnas are always better than one

S. Bartlett

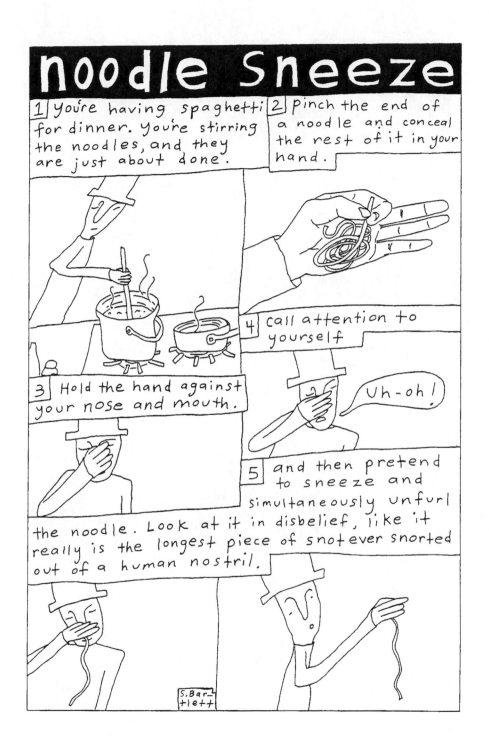

Clothespin Facial

This stunt does not play craftily along the subtle outer edge of disgusting; it plunges instead into the epicenter of the repulsive. From Bob Duffy of Indianapolis, we have the

KETCHUP/COLA REVERSAL STUNT

Scenario: you're at a fast food "restaurant" with a friend. They have a cola or some other kind of soft drink. There is a little package of ketchup lingering innocently on the table. Your friend gets up to go to the bathroom.

OK

I'll be back in just a minute

As soon as they disappear, you flip the lid and the straw combo off the drink.

Then you make a little hole in the ketchup thingy and fit the ketchup package over the end of the straw -- the end that will go back into the cola

ketchup

Do you follow me? Are you gagging? The next step naturally is to stick the straw with the ketchup on it <u>back</u> into the drink, and then wait for friend to come back and take his/her first thirsty pull on the soft drink straw. You should be prepared to buy your friend a fresh drink, although this stunt done correctly will not contaminate the beverage. The stunt works nicely with milkshakes, I would imagine. I find this stunt exceptionally vile. Thanks Bob!

S. Bartlett

95

97

Fake Math Stunt
1
1 1
2 1
1 2 1 1
1 1 1 2 2 1
3 1 2 2 1 1
?
This is a fake math stunt because it seems to be a numerical sequence that you derive by the trickeries of mathematical calculations. But, in fact, it is not.
To start, you present someone with this group of numbers and you ask, "What is the next logical sequence, given the relationships presented here?"
They will begin rifling through their brain, attempting all sorts of mathematical gymnastics to crack the code. And maybe they'll even find a mathematical answer. But the beauty of the sequence is...
You can solve it verbally! To solve it, you must simply say what you see. Each line, other than the first, describes the line before it, if read aloud.
1 one one
1 1 two ones
2 1 one two one one
1 2 1 1 one one one two two ones
1 1 1 2 2 1 three ones two twos one one
3 1 2 2 1 1
So the next sequence in frame #1 would be:
1 3 1 1 2 2 2 1
from Erika Biga
S. Bartlett

HAIR TONIC

Start by grabbing your cheeks in a pinch grip. Use index fingers and thumbs.

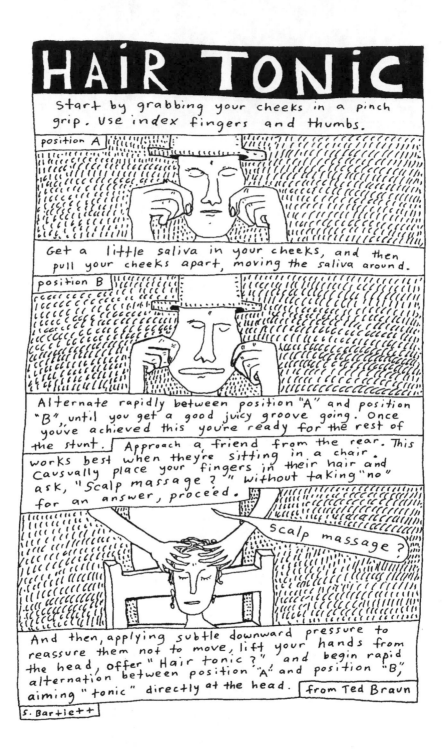

position A

Get a little saliva in your cheeks, and then pull your cheeks apart, moving the saliva around.

position B

Alternate rapidly between position "A" and position "B" until you get a good juicy groove going. Once you've achieved this you're ready for the rest of the stunt. Approach a friend from the rear. This works best when they're sitting in a chair. Casually place your fingers in their hair and ask, "Scalp massage?" Without taking "no" for an answer, proceed.

Scalp massage?

And then, applying subtle downward pressure to reassure them not to move, lift your hands from the head, offer "Hair tonic?" and begin rapid alternation between position "A" and position "B," aiming "tonic" directly at the head.

from Ted Braun

S. Bartlett

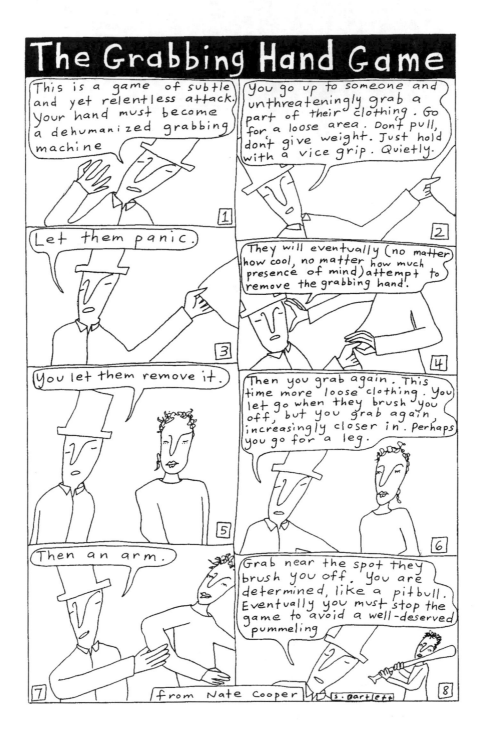

NOSEHAIR PLUCKING

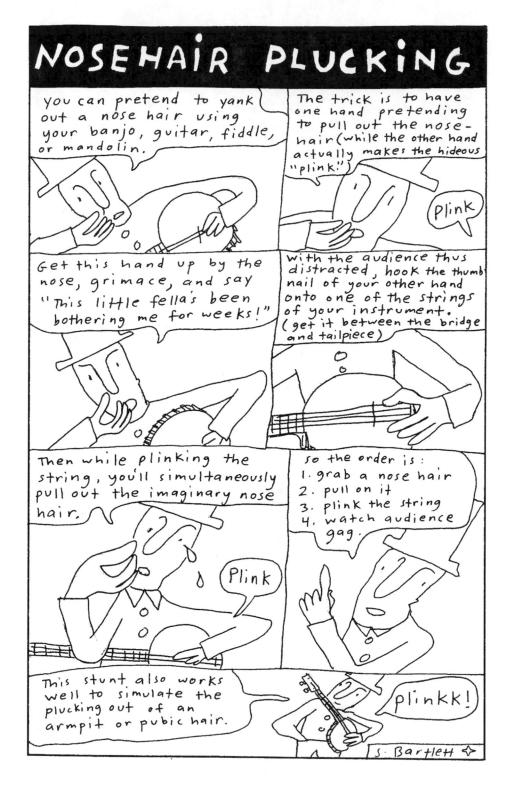

TABLE-LIFTING STUNT

from David Howells   S. Bartlett

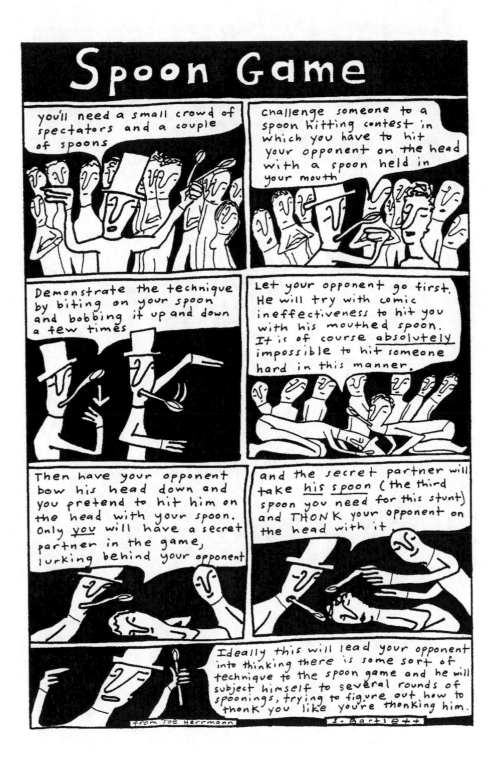

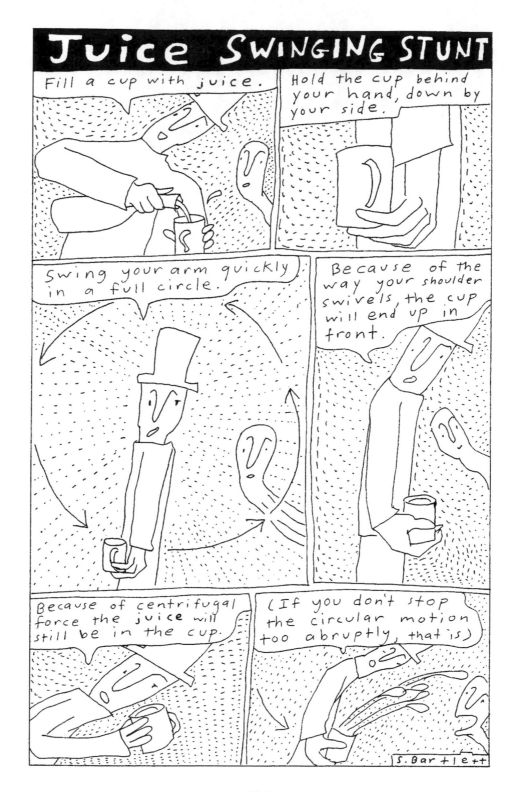

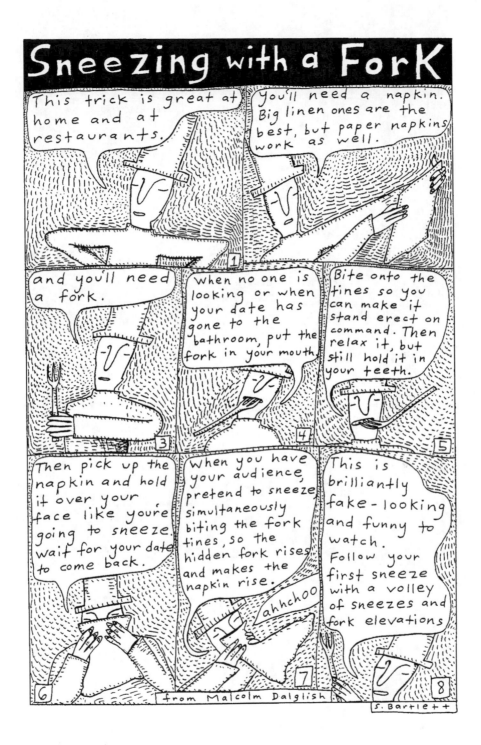

Sideways Spitting

I saw my friend Jimmy Leary invent and perfect this when we were eight.

It evolved naturally enough from regular spitting, which we were doing quite a lot of.

Regular spitting: straight out of the mouth

Sideways spitting simply involves moving the spitting orifice to one side of the mouth...

..and then spitting

The advantage of sideways spitting for Jimmy as I recall was that he could be having a conversation face to face with someone and spit without moving his head away from the person he was talking to.

Because of obvious risks involved with sideways spitting, I suggest you practice the following:

place your hand in front of your mouth, shift spitting orifice to one side, and blow air

you shouldn't feel the blowing on your hand. when you're good at blowing, move to spitting.

s.bartlett

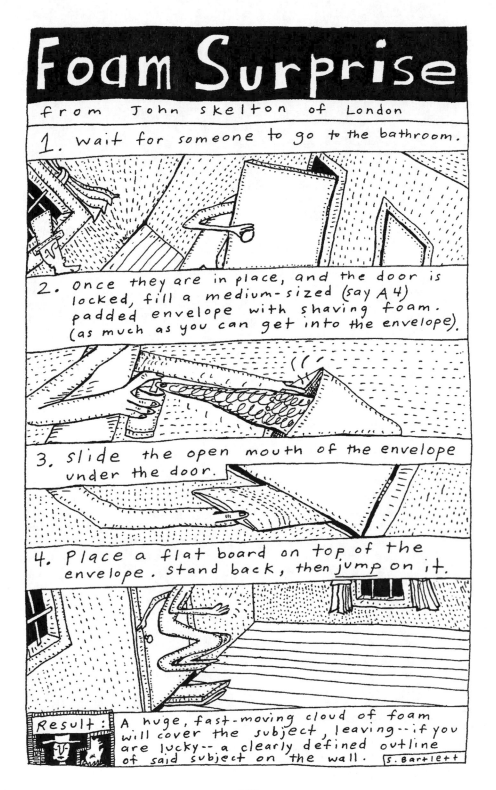

Foam Surprise

from John skelton of London

1. wait for someone to go to the bathroom.

2. Once they are in place, and the door is locked, fill a medium-sized (say A4) padded envelope with shaving foam. (as much as you can get into the envelope).

3. slide the open mouth of the envelope under the door.

4. Place a flat board on top of the envelope. stand back, then jump on it.

Result: A huge, fast-moving cloud of foam will cover the subject, leaving--if you are lucky-- a clearly defined outline of said subject on the wall. [S. Bartlett]

Index